Vegetarian Vi

RELATED TITLES PUBLISHED BY JON CARPENTER

Party Food for Vegetarians, Linda Majzlik
Animal Rights, Mark Gold
Caught in the Act! Melody MacDonald
Living Without Cruelty Diary, Mark Gold (annual)

Vegetarian Visitor 1997

Edited by Annemarie Weitzel

Jon Carpenter

to Shetlands

This edition first published 1997 by
Jon Carpenter Publishing, The Spendlove Centre, Charlbury, Oxfordshire OX7 3PQ
Tel and fax: 01608 811969
This compilation © Annemarie Weitzel
Whilst the publishers must disclaim responsibility for any inaccuracy, the information in
this guide has been carefully checked at the time of going to press
ISBN 1 897766 27 0
Printed and bound by J W Arrowsmith Ltd., Bristol, England

Contents

Introduction

Welcome to the 1997 edition of *Vegetarian Visitor*, listing private houses, guest houses, hotels, cafés, restaurants and pubs which take catering for vegetarians seriously. For the first time this year we are also indicating which establishments cater for vegans, whether they are licensed, and in the case of accommodation addresses whether they have disabled access. All establishments in this year's guide have been supplied with a 'We're in Vegetarian Visitor 1997' sticker, to make them easily recognisable.

How to use this guide

Entries are grouped geographically in sections. Within each section they are arranged alphabetically by county, then town, then name of establishment.

Accommodation addresses have coded information as well as a general description. The codes provide the following:

H Hotel   **G** Guesthouse   **PH** Private house

L Licensed

DA Disabled access

V Exclusively vegetarian: entries without this code also provide non-vegetarian fare

Ve Also catering for vegans. Please mention you are a vegan when you contact the establishment

Vegan Exclusively vegan

NS No smoking anywhere on the premises

pNS Smoking restricted to certain areas only

CN Car necessary: a car/taxi journey or extended walk is needed from the nearest public transport

Acc2 Accommodation for two adults. Children travelling with their parents can sometimes be included additionally.

Price categories for bed and breakfast per person per night (rough guide only): **CatA** over £25 **CatB** £16-£25 **CatC** under £16

Cafés, restaurants and pubs in many cases have a short description, as well as coded information. Opening times can vary not only by establishment, but also by season. As a general rule, cafés will be open during the day but not in the evening, and are often closed on Sundays and Bank holidays. Restaurants are generally open for lunch and in the evening; they may be closed one day a week, but this is not usually on Sunday. Pubs are normally open seven days a week and may be open all day and in the evening. If you want to be sure that your chosen eating place is open, please give them a ring. The codes give the following information:

R Restaurant   **C** Café   **P** Pub

L Licensed

a A selection of vegetarian dishes as well as non-vegetarian food

b Vegetarian food only

c Vegetarian and vegan food only

d Vegan food only

w Wholefood

NS No smoking anywhere on the premises

pNS Smoking restricted to certain areas only

I would be delighted to hear from any user of the guide and give any further help I can. If you have any suggestions, or have stayed or eaten anywhere that is not in the guide, please drop me a line. Have a happy stay in Vegetarian Britain!

Annemarie Weitzel, 2 Home Farm Cottages, Sandy Lane, St Paul's Cray, Kent BR5 3HZ: phone/fax 01689 870437

Dafs Guesthouse, Swansea (see pp 9 and 54).

Activity holidays
Courses
Nationwide holidays

Countrywide Holidays
☎ 0161 446 2226, fax 0161 448 7113

Grove House, Wilmslow Road, Didsbury, Manchester M20 2HU

Walking holidays and guest houses throughout the country offering vegetarian cuisine. See display ad on page 26.

Dafs Guesthouse
☎ and fax 01792 475731

116 Bryn Road, Brynmill, Swansea SA2 0AT

Brush up your English. Multilingual hostess/teacher (German/French/Italian) offers two hours of conversation a day. For further details see page 54.

Minton House
☎ 01309 690819, fax 01309 691583

Findhorn, Moray IV36 0YY

Retreats and workshops. For further details see page 58.

The Old Court House Vegetarian Guest House
☎ 01348 837095

Trefin, near St Davids, Pembrokeshire SA62 5AX

Self-guided walking holidays and climbing activities. For further details see page 56.

Shepherd's Purse (see page 41).

London and Middlesex

Central London

• *Cafés, restaurants, pubs*

Carnevale ☎ 0171 250 3452
135 Whitecross Street, London EC1Y 8JL   R L c

Food For Thought ☎ 0171 836 9072/0239, fax 0171 379 1249
31 Neal Street, Covent Garden, London WC2H 9PA
Award-winning vegetarian restaurant: lively atmosphere, exceptional
food at edible prices (main meals from £2.70 inc). BYOs welcome (no
corkage).   R c NS

Greenhouse Vegetarian Restaurant ☎ 0171 637 8038
16 Chenies Street, London WC1E 7EX   R c NS

Leith's at the Natural History Museum ☎ 0171 938 8149
NHM, Cromwell Road, London SW7 5BD   R/C L a NS

Mildreds ☎ 0171 494 1634
58 Greek Street, London W1V 5LR   R/C L c w NS

Sri Siam Soho ☎ 0171 434 3544
16 Old Compton Street, Soho, London W1V 5PE   R L a

Windmill Restaurant ☎ 0171 381 2372
486 Fulham Road, Fulham, London SW6 5NJ
An exciting menu, changing daily. Open 11am-11pm 7 days a week
for lunch and dinner. Breakfast served on weekends from 10am.
                                                  R L c w pNS

East London

• *Cafés, restaurants, pubs*

Cherry Orchard Vegetarian Restaurant ☎ 0181 980 6678
241 Globe Road, Bethnal Green, London E2 0JD   R c pNS

North London

Mrs M. Draper ☎ 0181 346 7985
31 The Ridgeway, Finchley, London N3 2PG

Bed and breakfast £15 per night, 1/2 hour from Central London.
Very quiet situation backing onto park. Separate kitchen if guests
wish to cook their own evening meal. Non-smoking. Plenty of
parking space.
PH CatC Ve NS Acc5+child

Dora Rothner ☎ 0181 346 0246
23 The Ridgeway, Finchley, London N3 2PG

Comfortable bedrooms in quiet friendly home, two double, one
single, with Z-bed for one extra if required. Attractive garden
overlooking park. Five minutes walk Finchley Central
Underground, twenty minutes to Central London. Will meet with
car from Finchley Central by arrangement.
PH CatC V Ve NS Acc5/6

• *Cafés, restaurants, pubs*

Clissold Park Café ☎ 0171 249 0672
   'The Mansion', Clissold Park, Stoke Newington Church Street,
   London N16 C c w pNS
Fatty Arbuckles American Diner ☎ 0171 609 6453
   385/401 Holloway Road, Islington, London N7 0RY R L a pNS
Fatty Arbuckles American Diner ☎ 0181 808 8848
   Ferry Island, Ferry Lane, Tottenham, London N17 9LR R L a pNS
The Greenhouse ☎ 0181 881 1471
   64-67 Market Hall, Wood Green Shopping Centre, London N22
   C c w pNS
Rani Vegetarian Restaurant ☎ 0181 349 4386
   7 Long Lane, Finchley, London N3 2PR R L c pNS

South London

Coonan   ☎ 0181 543 2607
22 Mayfield Road, Wimbledon, London SW19 3NF

In artists' detached home, twin- and single-bedded rooms with own bathroom. British Rail main line station, South Wimbledon and Wimbledon Underground stations 12 minutes' walk. Canadians particularly welcome. Off street parking.
PH CatB Ve pNS Acc3

West London

Temple Lodge   ☎ 0181 748 8388
51 Queen Caroline Street, Hammersmith, London W6 9QL

Listed Georgian house with twin-bedded rooms, each with hand-basin. Continental breakfast, vegetarian restaurant on premises (closed Sundays). Large secluded garden, riverbank walks nearby. Handy for Heathrow, Kew, West End, etc. via Underground.
G CatB V Ve pNS Acc12

Middlesex

• *Cafés, restaurants, pubs*

Fatty Arbuckles American Diner ☎ 0181 861 0007
26 St George's Shopping & Leisure Centre, St Ann's Road, Harrow HA1 1HS   R L a pNS

Percy's Restaurant ☎ 0181 427 2021
66-68 Station Road, North Harrow HA2 7SJ   R L a NS

South and South East

Dorset

St Antoine ☎ 01202 433043
2 Guildhill Road, Southbourne, Bournemouth BH6 3EY

Family-run, well-established guest house. Good home cooking. Comfy rooms with wash hand-basins and tea/coffee making facilities. Two family en-suite rooms. Close to beach, sports facilities, river walks. On bus route for town centre.
G CatB Ve NS Acc17

The Orchard ☎ 01929 400592
West Road, West Lulworth BH20 5RY (Lulworth Cove)

Peaceful location, yet central, set back from road in old vicarage orchard. Safe parking in spacious walled garden with views of Purbeck Hills. Close to restaurants and village pub. Cove, coastal paths and beaches nearby. Generous vegetarian, vegan or traditional English breakfasts. Open all year.
PH CatC Ve pNS Acc5

• *Cafés, restaurants, pubs*
Fatty Arbuckles American Diner ☎ 01202 293355
  148 Old Christchurch Road, Bournemouth BH1 1NL   R L a pNS
Fatty Arbuckles American Diner ☎ 01202 669747
  3 High Street, Poole BH15 1BP   R L a pNS

Hampshire

• *Cafés, restaurants, pubs*
Country Kitchen at Havant Arts Centre ☎ 01705 480113
  Old Town Hall, East Street, Havant PO9 1BS
  Enjoy a triple experience – arts centre and museum in the same building, as well as the locally renowned bakes and soups, teas and

coffee. Open Monday-Saturday 9.30-4.30, plus some speciality
evenings.   R L c w NS

Fatty Arbuckles American Diner ☎ 01703 223153
20 Bedford Place, Southampton SO1 2BX   R L a pNS
Country Kitchen ☎ 01705 811425
59 Marmion Road, Southsea PO5 2AX
Renowned for delicious savoury bakes, divine steaming soups and
unique quiches, all made daily on the premises. Speciality teas, free
refill coffee and take-away service. Open Monday-Saturday 9.30-5.
                                                     R c w NS
Fatty Arbuckles American Diner ☎ 01705 739179
61 Osborne Road, Southsea PO5 3LS   R L a pNS

Isle of Wight

The Ryde Castle Hotel   ☎ 01983 563755
The Esplanade, Ryde, Isle of Wight PO33 1JA
See display ad on page 16.
H CatA L Ve pNS Acc36

The Edgecliffe Hotel   ☎ and fax 01983 866199
**7 Clarence Gardens, Shanklin, Isle of Wight PO37
6HA**
A charming, friendly hotel close to the famous cliff top walk,
comfortably furnished and tastefully decorated. All rooms have
hairdryers, TVs and radios, tea making facilities, most are en-
suite. Combined bar/dining room, separate TV lounge. Very
varied vegetarian menu. Special diets by arrangement. Children
welcome. No pets. Open all year.
H CatB L NS CN Acc25

Strang Hall   ☎ 01983 753189
Uplands, Totland Bay, Isle of Wight PO39 0DZ
Strang Hall is an Edwardian family home with beautiful views of

15

Headon Warren and the Solent. An ideal base to explore the West Wight and beyond. We enjoy cooking suppers, and picnics (by prior arrangement please). Four bedrooms, all with views.
PH CatB Ve pNS CN Acc6

Kent

Roydon Hall
☎ 01622 812121, fax 01622 813959
East Peckham, Tonbridge TN12 5NH

Beautiful sixteenth-century manor in ten acres of woodlands and gardens. Peaceful atmosphere, magnificent views. Single, double and family rooms available, all centrally heated, with or without en-suite facilities. Less than one hour from central London, Dover, and the south coast.
G CatC V Ve NS CN Acc45

16

Roydon Hall, Kent (see page 16)

• *Cafés, restaurants, pubs*

Fatty Arbuckles American Diner ☎ 01227 784770
45 St Peters Street, Canterbury CT1 2BH R L a pNS

Fungus Mungus ☎ 01227 781922
34 St Peters Street, Canterbury
A relaxed environment in an excellent location, with outdoor seating
and regular music nights. Draught beers, twenty-five country wines.
C/P L c pNS

The India Restaurant ☎ 01303 259155
1 The Old High Street, (Rendezvous Street), Folkestone CT20 1RJ
'The best Indian restaurant in South East England' – TVS. French and
German spoken. R L c

Surrey

• *Cafés, restaurants, pubs*

Hockneys Vegetarian Restaurant ☎ 0181 688 2899
98 High Street, Croydon CR0 1ND R c NS

17

The Riverside Vegetaria ☎ 0181 546 7992
64 High Street, Kingston KT1 1HN   R L c pNS
Rani Vegetarian Restaurant ☎ 0181 332 2322
3 Hill Street, Richmond TW9 1SX   R L c pNS
Fatty Arbuckles American Diner ☎ 01483 728013
1 Chertsey Road, Woking GU21 5AD   R L a pNS

Sussex

Paskins Town House Hotel

☎ 01273 601203, fax 01273 621973
19 Charlotte Street, Brighton BN2 1AG

A stylish Regency Hotel, environmentally friendly, providing vegetarian and organic food. Our vegetarian or traditional English breakfasts are delicious and tastefully decorated rooms make your stay a pleasure. Room prices between £15 and £30 p.p.p.n. Special break prices for vegetarians.
H CatC L Ve Acc35

Jeake's House

Mermaid Street, Rye, East Sussex TN31 7ET

☎ Rye (01797) 222828

Beautiful listed building built in 1689. Set in mediaeval cobblestoned street, renowned for its smuggling associations. Breakfast – served in eighteenth century galleried former chapel – is traditional or vegetarian. Oak-beamed and panelled bedrooms overlook the marsh and roof-tops to the sea. Brass, mahogany or four-poster beds, linen sheets and lace. En-suite bathrooms, hot drinks trays, direct dial telephones and televisions. Four-poster honeymoon suite and family room available. Residential licence.

AA QQQQQ Premier Selected   RAC Highly Acclaimed   Cesar Award 1992

Write or telephone for further details to the proprietors:
Mr & Mrs F. Hadfield
Fax: (01797) 222623

Jeake's House   ☎ 01797 222828
Mermaid Street, Rye, East Sussex TN31 7ET
See display ad on page 18.
G CatB L Ve pNS Acc25

• *Cafés, restaurants, pubs*
Corianders   ☎ 01424 220329
> 66 Devonshire Road, Bexhill-on-Sea, East Sussex TN40 1AX
> Bexhill town centre. Everything made on the premises, guaranteed
> 100% wholemeal and vegetarian. Pastries and cakes our speciality,
> plus lunchtime menu.   R L c w pNS

Rhododendrons create a blaze of spring colour in the Surrey hills.

West Country

Cornwall

Woodstock

☎ and fax 01736 369049

29 Morrab Road, Penzance TR18 4EZ

Victorian guest house in central Penzance. Ideally situated for
walking coastal path and visiting local beaches, coves and villages.
Close to bus and rail stations. Most rooms en-suite. AA*QQQ*, RAC.
G CatB DA pNS Acc14

Tremore

☎ 01872 573537

Liskey Hill Crescent, Perranporth TR6 0HP

A warm welcome awaits you in our well-established and highly
recommended guest house. Non-smoking. Full vegetarian
breakfasts. Four minutes' walk to beach. Off-road parking. Ideal
for touring. Excellent value. Try us, you won't be disappointed:
satisfaction guaranteed.
G CatB Ve NS Acc6

The Grey Mullet

☎ 01736 796635

2 Bunkers Hill, St Ives TR26 1LJ

Relax in a beautiful eighteenth-century Cornish house with oak
beams, antiques, paintings, comfortable lounge with open fire.
Cosy en-suite bedrooms. Ideal harbour position to enjoy art
galleries – including the Tate – cliff walks and beaches. Varied
breakfast menu. ETB 2 Crown Commended.
G CatB Ve pNS Acc13

Making Waves Vegan Guest House

☎ 01736 793895

3 Richmond Place, St Ives TR26 1JN

Delightful Victorian house with stunning views of St Ives Bay and

sub-tropical gardens. Sunny patio and wild garden. Relaxed, friendly atmosphere. Two minutes' stroll to town centre and picturesque harbour, ten minutes to four glorious beaches and Tate Gallery. Food is 100% animal-free and mostly organic, with the emphasis on health and nutrition. Special diets catered for. Children most welcome.
G CatC Vegan pNS Acc6

• *Cafés, restaurants, pubs*

Fox & Hounds Inn ☎ 01209 820205
  Scorrier, Redruth TR16 5BS   P L a pNS
The Thin End ☎ 01726 75805
  41A Fore Street, St Austell PL25 5PY   C L a pNS
The Feast ☎ 01872 72546
  15 Kenwyn Street, Truro TR1 3BU   R L c w pNS

Devon

The Bear Hotel
☎ 01598 753391

Lydiate Lane, Lynton, North Devon EX35 6AJ

See display ad on page 21.

H CatB L Ve pNS Acc18

South Sands Hotel

☎ 01803 557231, fax 01803 529947

12 Alta Vista Road, Goodrington Sands, Paignton, South Devon TQ4 6BZ

Linda McCartney eat your heart out. Outstanding home-cooked cuisine. Family-run, 3 Crown Commended, 200 yards golden sands/large park. Quiet area, beautiful greenery. Short walk to town/harbour. Many amenities. Large car park. Informal, friendly, relaxed. Nutritious, delicious, don't miss us.

H CatB L DA pNS Acc56

Allington House
☎ 01752 221435

6 St James Place East, The Hoe, Plymouth PL1 3AS

An elegant Victorian town house situated in a secluded square between shopping centre and Hoe Promenade. Clean, comfortable bedrooms with wash basin, beverage facilities, television and central heating. En-suite rooms available. A full English breakfast is included. Brittany Ferries recommended.

G CatB Ve pNS Acc8

Sunningdale
☎ 01548 843513

Main Road, Salcombe TQ8 8JW

A 1930s style house in a lovely position, with views over estuary and countryside. Large garden. Dogs welcome! Also available self-catering flat, sleeps four, cot, very well equipped.

PH CatB Ve NS CN Acc6

Brocklehurst Hotel

☎ 0500 505450 (freephone), fax 01803 213795

E-mail Brockle@aol.Com

Rathmore Road, Torquay TQ2 6NZ

A warm welcome awaits you.
Relax, enjoy our personal
attention and delicious food.
Family run since 1977. Five
minutes level walk to station and
the main beach. 3 Crown luxury
– warm cosy bar – en-suite rooms
with Sky television. Dinner, B&B
from £26 per person per night.
H CatB L DA Ve pNS Acc26

• *Cafés, restaurants, pubs*

The National Trust Restaurants and Tea Rooms in Devon

Arlington Court ☎ 01271 850629	
Arlington, Barnstaple EX31 4LP	R L a NS
Buckland Abbey ☎ 01822 853607	
Nr Yelverton PL20 6EY	R L a NS
Castle Drogo ☎ 01647 432629	
Drewsteignton, Exeter EX6 6PB	R L a NS
Killerton House ☎ 01392 882081	
Broadclyst, Exeter EX5 3LF	R L a NS
Knightshayes Court ☎ 01884 259416	
The Stable Block, Bolham, Tiverton EX16 7RQ	R L a NS
Lydford Gorge ☎ 0182282 441	
Lydford, Okehampton EX20 4BH	C a NS
Overbecks Museum & Garden ☎ 0154884 2893	
Sharpitor, Salcombe TQ8 8LW	C a NS
Saltram House ☎ 01752 340635	
Plympton, Plymouth PL7 3UH	R L a NS
Watersmeet House ☎ 01598 53348	
Lynton EX35 6NT	C a NS

The Devon Guild of Craftsmen ☎ 01626 832223
Riverside Mill, Bovey Tracey TQ13 9AF
Café, shop and gallery selling work of members, who include the very
best makers in the South West. Open 10am-5pm.   C L a NS
Herbies ☎ 01392 58473
15 North Street, Exeter EX4 3QS   R L c w pNS
The Peter Tavy Inn ☎ 01822 810348
Peter Tavy, Tavistock PL19 9NN   P L a w pNS
See display ad below.
Willow Vegetarian Restaurant ☎ 01803 862605
87 High Street, Totnes TQ9 5PB   R L c w NS
Percy's at Coombeshead ☎ 01409 211275
Virginstow EX21 5EA   R L a NS

Somerset and Bristol

Tyning House
☎ 01225 723288

Freshford Lane, Freshford, Bath BA3 6DR

Large Victorian house and coachhouse with four self-catering apartments (ETB 4 Key Commended) and two B&B double rooms, set in seven acres organically run grounds. Hard tennis court, produce, rare breeds and domestic animals to enjoy. Lovely walks, beautiful countryside, peaceful and welcoming venue. Bath 6 miles.
G CatB DA Ve CN Acc8

Merefield Vegetarian Guest House
☎ 01460 73112

East Street, Crewkerne TA18 7AB

Spacious Grade II listed house in historic town of Crewkerne. Serving imaginative vegetarian cuisine with seasonal home-grown produce. An ideal base for walking, touring N.T. gardens, or just relaxing in our walled gardens and large guest lounge.
G CatB V Ve pNS Acc6

Exmoor Lodge
☎ 01643 831694

Chapel Street, Exford TA24 7PY

In the heart of Exmoor National Park, overlooking Exford village green, combining cruelty-free principles with healthy food. A set three course evening meal is prepared fresh each day by the 'Cordon Vert' qualified proprietor. Most rooms en-suite.
G CatB V Ve NS CN Acc9

Rosemullion
☎ 01458 831182

54 Roman Way, Glastonbury BA6 8AD

Attractive, quiet house, surrounded by trees, set on Wearyall Hill. Short walk from Holy Thorn. Some rooms with hand-basins. Family room with double bed and bunk beds (reductions for

children). Also group bookings/courses with optional catering.
Conference room.
PH CatB DA Vegan NS Acc8-14

Doverhay Place   ☎ 01643 862996
Porlock, Minehead TA24 8EX

See display ad below.
G CatB L Ve pNS Acc45

The Royal Ashton Hotel   ☎ 01823 272456
Station Road, Taunton TA1 1PD

Centrally located family-run hotel close to town centre, cricket
ground and main line station. All rooms en-suite with tea/coffee
making, colour TV and telephone. Full central heating. All day
café bar and restaurant. Entertainment lounge.
H CatA L Ve Acc40

• Cafés, restaurants, pubs

Demuths Vegetarian Restaurant ☎ 01225 446059
2 North Parade Passage, Bath BA1 1NX
http://www.gold.net/amoz/users/demuth.html.
Demuths provides innovative vegetarian cuisine. Daily changing lunch
and evening menus. Plenty of vegan options. Totally organic wine list.

R L c NS

Sally Lunn's Refreshment House ☎ 01225 461634
4 North Parade Passage, Bath BA1 1NX   R/C L a NS
Tilleys Bistro ☎ 01225 484200
3 North Parade Passage, Bath BA1 1NX   R L a pNS
The Wife of Bath Restaurant ☎ 01225 461745
Pierrepont Street, Bath BA1 1LA
Attractive, popular bistro with a long tradition of highly-praised
vegetarian dishes. Children welcome, pretty patio for summer, private
rooms for party bookings.   R L a pNS
Michaels Restaurant ☎ 0117 927 6190
129 Hotwell Road, Bristol BS8 4RU   R L a pNS
Millwards ☎ 0117 924 5026
40 Alfred Place, Kingsdown, Bristol BS2 8HD   R L c NS

Wiltshire

Bradford Old Windmill   ☎ 01225 866842
4 Masons Lane, Bradford on Avon BA15 1QN
'A little touch of romance near Bath' in an old windmill.
Dramatic position above an old Cotswold stone town with
spectacular views. Vegetarian/vegan breakfast. Exclusively
vegetarian/vegan dinner from around the world – Caribbean,
Thai, Nepali (Monday, Thursday, Saturday only).
G CatA Ve NS CN Acc8

• Cafés, restaurants, pubs

Stones Restaurant ☎ 01672 539514
Avebury, Marlborough SN8 1RF   R/C L c w pNS

Thames and Chilterns

Bedfordshire

• *Cafés, restaurants, pubs*

Fatty Arbuckles American Diner ☎ 01234 340044
Aspects Leisure Centre, Newnham Avenue, Bedford MK41 9LW
R L a pNS

Berkshire

• *Cafés, restaurants, pubs*

The Harrow ☎ 01635 281260
West Ilsley, Newbury RG20 7AR
P L a pNS

Buckinghamshire

• *Cafés, restaurants, pubs*

The Peking Restaurant ☎ 01908 563120
117 High Street, Stony Stratford, Milton Keynes MK11 1AT
R L a pNS

Hertfordshire

• *Cafés, restaurants, pubs*

Fatty Arbuckles American Diner ☎ 01707 267548
Unit 6a, Galleria, Comet Way, Hatfield AL10 0XR   R L a pNS
The Waffle House ☎ 01727 853502
Kingsbury Watermill, St Michael's Street, St Albans AL3 4SJ
Restaurant set in Elizabethan Watermill Museum building, specialising
in waffles with savoury and sweet toppings. Open Tuesday-Saturday
11am-6pm, Sunday 12-6pm, closed Monday except Bank Holidays.
R a w NS

Oxfordshire

• *Cafés, restaurants, pubs*

Frageo's ☎ 01235 523260
2 East St Helen Street, Abingdon OX14 5EA C L a w NS

The Coffee House ☎ 01608 811414
11 Sheep Street, Charlbury OX7 3RR C a NS

Browns Restaurant ☎ 01865 511995
5-11 Woodstock Road, Oxford OX2 6HA R L a pNS

Fatty Arbuckles American Diner ☎ 01865 201899
Threeways House, St Georges Place, Gloucester Green, Oxford OX1 2BG R L a pNS

Hi Lo Jamaican Eating House ☎ 01865 725984
68-70 Cowley Road, Oxford OX4 1JB
Delicious meals and snacks. Tropical fruits and vegetables. Organic ices. Jamaican drinks. Relaxed atmosphere. Children welcome. Also shop. R/C L a w pNS

Café M.O.M.A. ☎ 01865 813814
Museum of Modern Art, 30 Pembroke Street, Oxford OX1 1BP
Great food, great coffees, great atmosphere! (Good art gallery too!)
Open Tuesday-Saturday 9-5.30 (Thursday to 9.30pm), Sunday 11-5.30. C L c w NS

Moonlight Tandoori Restaurant ☎ 01865 240275
56-60 Cowley Road, Oxford OX4 1JB R L a pNS

The Nosebag Restaurant ☎ 01865 721033
6-8 St Michael's Street, Oxford OX1 2DU R L a NS

Vale & Downland Museum ☎ 01235 771447
Church Street, Wantage OX12 8BL C a NS

The Country Pie ☎ 01993 703590
63 Corn Street, Witney OX8 7DQ
A sixteenth-century Cotswold building. Here, good food is served in congenial surroundings with an air of calm efficiency. R L a pNS

Beside the Thames and a short walk from Oxford, Iffley village boasts a fine Norman church and a popular riverside pub.

East Anglia

Cambridgeshire

• *Cafés, restaurants, pubs*

Free Press Public House ☎ 01223 368337
  Prospect Row, Cambridge CB1 1DU
  Small Victorian pub near the Grafton Centre specialising in real ale
  and good food with a friendly, smoke-free atmosphere.   P L a NS

Hobbs Pavilion Restaurant ☎ 01223 367480
  Park Terrace, Cambridge CB1 1JH
  Both vegetarian and vegan pancakes, savoury or sweet. All food
  prepared from fresh in our kitchen. Closed Sundays and Mondays.
  R L a NS

The Old Ferry Boat Inn ☎ 01480 463227
  Holywell, nr St Ives PE17 3TG   P L a pNS

Essex

• *Cafés, restaurants, pubs*

Scott's ☎ 01245 380161
  The Street, Hatfield Peverel, Chelmsford CM3 2DR   R L a NS

Fatty Arbuckles American Diner ☎ 01702 338712
  33/35 Alexandra Street, Southend-on-Sea SS9 1LG   R L a pNS

Norfolk

Meadow House   ☎ 01328 830551
Walsingham Road, Binham NR21 0BU

Get away from it all, come to our comfortable house surrounded
by peaceful countryside, three miles beautiful North Norfolk
coastline. Guests' sitting room with log fire, pleasant bedrooms
and a hearty vegetarian breakfast. Evening meals by arrangement.
Phone Helen for details.
PH CatB V NS CN Acc4

• Cafés, restaurants, pubs

The Kings Arms Hotel ☎ 01263 740341
Blakeney, Holt NR25 7NQ   P L a pNS
The Treehouse ☎ 01603 763258
14 Dove Street, Norwich NR2 1DE   C L c w NS

Dry stone walls and isolated barns are features of the landscape of the
Yorkshire and Derbyshire dales

East Midlands

Derbyshire

Riber Hall
☎ 01629 582795
Matlock DE4 5JU

Enjoy pure tranquillity and outstanding cuisine in this historic Derbyshire Country House, recently nominated as 'One of the most romantic hotels in Britain' and recommended by all major hotel and restaurant guides. Two-day breaks available. Open daily for luncheon and dinner. M1 exit 28, 20 minutes.
H CatA L Ve pNS CN Acc24

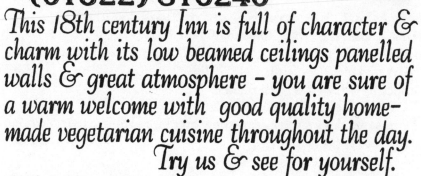

Leicestershire

- *Cafés, restaurants, pubs*

Fatty Arbuckles American Diner ☎ 0116 289 4116
  Meridian Leisure Park, Lubbesthorpe Way, Leicester LE3 2JZ

R L a pNS

Lincolnshire

The Bell Inn
☎ 01522 810240

Far Lane, Coleby LN5 0AH

See display ad on page 33.
G CatB Ve CN Acc6

The Waveney Guest House
☎ 01673 843236

Willingham Road, Market Rasen LN8 3DN

Highly recommended for comfort, cleanliness and home-cooked food, Waveney is run by ex-H.E. teacher with Heartbeat Award 1995. All rooms en-suite with tea making equipment and colour TV. Guests own lounge and dining room. Pets welcome. Open all year.
G CatC Ve NS Acc6

- *Cafés, restaurants, pubs*

Fatty Arbuckles American Diner ☎ 01472 251700
  Unit 2, Osborne Street, Grimsby DN31 1EY   R L a pNS
Mantles Fish & Chips ☎ 01507 526726
  Market Place, Horncastle LN9 5BJ   R L a pNS
Tuppenny Rice ☎ 01780 62739
  1 Castle Street, Stamford PE9 2RA
  Open seven days a week, plus some evenings with live music. Phone for details!   C c w NS

Nottinghamshire

• *Cafés, restaurants, pubs*

Gannets Café ☎ 01636 702066
  35 Castlegate, Newark NG24 1AZ   R L a w NS
Maxine's Salad Table ☎ 0115 947 3622
  56/58 Upper Parliament Street, Nottingham NG1 2AG
                                                   C L c w pNS

Sandy coves, rocks and cliff walks are among the attractions of the Welsh
coastline in Cardigan Bay.

Heart of England

Gloucestershire

Charlton House
☎ and fax 01242 238997

**18 Greenhills Road, Charlton Kings, Cheltenham
GL53 9EB**

Ideal touring base for the beautiful Cotswolds in a Regency spa
town. Excellent accommodation, some en-suite rooms. ETB 2
Crown Highly Commended, AA 4Q quality rating. All diets
catered for by trained cook and nutritionist. Evening meals by
arrangement. Ample off road parking. Reductions for 3 days.
Entirely non-smoking.
G CatB Ve NS Acc5

Cherry Grove
☎ 01989 720126

Mill Lane, Kilcot, Newent GL18 1NY

Centrally heated, family-run B&B in peaceful rural situation
convenient to Forest of Dean, Wye Valley, Gloucester. One en-
suite room on ground floor. Ample parking, locked cycle shed,
tea/coffee facilities, TV available. No pets allowed. ETB listed.
PH CatC NS CN Acc6

• *Cafés, restaurants, pubs*

The Baytree ☎ 01242 516229
  Regent Arcade, Cheltenham GL50 1JZ   C a pNS
Below Stairs Restaurant ☎ 01242 234599
  103 Promenade, Cheltenham GL50 1NW   R a pNS
The Edgemoor Inn ☎ 01452 813576
  Edge, Stroud GL6 6ND   R/P L a pNS
The Ragged Cot Inn ☎ 01453 731333
  Cirencester Road, Hyde, nr Stroud GL6 8PC   P L a pNS

Herefordshire

The Poplars   ☎ 01981 240516
Ewyas Harold HR2 0HU

Stay with us and relax in a friendly atmosphere. Good walking, castles and churches close to the lovely Black Mountains. Home-cooked evening meal by arrangement. German, Spanish and French spoken.
PH CatC V Ve NS CN Acc5

• *Cafés, restaurants, pubs*
'Nutters' ☎ 01432 277447
  Capuchin Yard, Church Street, Hereford HR1 2LT   C L c w pNS

Shropshire

The Old Bake House   ☎ 01299 270193
46/47 High Street, Cleobury Mortimer, nr Kidderminster DY14 8DQ

Grade II listed Georgian town house situated in the centre of Cleobury Mortimer. Comfortable bedrooms with en-suite/private facilities, residents' lounge. Evening meals available and diets catered for. A good centre for National Trust, English Heritage, Offa's Dyke and walking.
PH CatB Ve pNS Acc6

• *Cafés, restaurants, pubs*
Acorn Wholefood Restaurant Coffee Shop ☎ 01694 722495
  26 Sandford Avenue, Church Stretton SY6 6BW   R/C L c w NS
The Courtyard ☎ 01584 878080
  2 Quality Square, Ludlow SY8 1AR   R L a pNS
Bear's Paw Restaurant ☎ 01691 652093
  Salop Road, Oswestry SY11 2NR   R L a
The Goodlife Restaurant ☎ 01743 350455
  Barracks Passage, Wyle Cop, Shrewsbury SY1 1XA   R L c w pNS

Staffordshire

• *Cafés, restaurants, pubs*

Fatty Arbuckles American Diner ☎ 01782 269779
  Festival Park, Etruria, Stoke-on-Trent ST1 5SF   R L a pNS

Warwickshire

Parkfield Guest House   ☎ 01789 293313

3 Broad Walk, Stratford-upon-Avon CV37 6HS

Charming Victorian house, quietly located a few minutes' walk
from theatres and restaurants. A good choice of breakfast
provided. En-suite rooms available. Central heating. Car park.
G CatB Ve NS Acc13

Winton House   ☎ 01789 720500, mobile 0831 485483

The Green, Upper Quinton, Stratford CV37 8SX

E-mail: lyong@ibm.net
Internet: http://www.demon.co.uk/quinsolve/winton.htm.
Historic 1856 farmhouse in area of outstanding natural beauty
convenient for touring, walking and cycling. Antique four-poster
beds, handmade quilts, log fires. Heartbeat Award winning
breakfasts. Cycles, pubs.
PH CatB NS CN Acc6

West Midlands

Merdeka   ☎ 01902 884775

16 Dawlish Road, Dudley DY1 4LU

Detached house in quiet area just off A 4123, with open aspect to
front. Close to Wrens Nest Nature Reserve with its archaeological
interest, 1 1/2 miles Blackcountry Museum, 1 mile town centre.
Warm welcome, home cooking, evening beverage and welcoming
tray, off road parking. Evening meals by arrangement.
PH CatC Ve NS Acc3

• Cafés, restaurants, pubs

Cornerstone Coffee Shop ☎ 0121 449 3324
25 Woodbridge Road, Moseley, Birmingham B13 8EH   C a NS
Fatty Arbuckles American Diner ☎ 0121 212 1880
Paradise Forum, Paradise Place, Birmingham B3 3HJ   R L a pNS
Fatty Arbuckles American Diner ☎ 0121 568 6910
Bentley Mill Way, Walsall WS2 0BP   R L a pNS

Worcestershire

Tytchney Gables   ☎ 01905 620185
Boreley, Ombersley WR9 0HZ

Sixteenth-
century
medieval Hall
House cottage
in peaceful
country lane,
2 1/2 miles
Ombersley,
8 miles
Worcester.

Ideal for walking and touring. River Severn nearby and just half a
mile to Ombersley Golf Course. Double, family and single rooms,
cot available. B&B from £14.
PH CatC Ve CN Acc6

• Cafés, restaurants, pubs

Brief Encounter ☎ 01684 893033
Great Malvern Station, Imperial Road, Malvern WR14 3AT
Gourmet vegetarian restaurant serving inspired and original food in a
friendly and romantic setting at Malvern's Victorian railway station.
       R L c NS
Lady Foleys Tearoom ☎ 01684 893033
Great Malvern Station, Imperial Road, Malvern WR14 3AT   C a NS

North East England

County Durham

• *Cafés, restaurants, pubs*

Priors ☎ 01833 638141
7 The Bank, Barnard Castle DL12 8PH
Fronted by contemporary fine art/crafts; special diets; organic wine
list; children's menu; nappy change; open 7 days; gourmet evenings.

R L c w NS

Stile Restaurant ☎ 01388 746615, fax 01388 747400
97 High Street, Willington, Crook DL15 0PE   R L a pNS

Northumberland

• *Cafés, restaurants, pubs*

Chantry Tea Rooms ☎ 01670 514414
9 Chantry Place, Morpeth NE61 1PJ   C L a NS

Tyne & Wear

• *Cafés, restaurants, pubs*

The Wildfowl & Wetlands Trust ☎ 0191 416 5454
District 15, Washington NE38 8LE
See display ad on page 41.   C L a NS

Yorkshire

Sansbury Place   ☎ 01729 823840
Duke Street, Settle, North Yorkshire BD24 9AS

Spacious Victorian house with splendid views of the surrounding
limestone scenery. Sample our imaginative vegetarian and special
diet cooking; relax in front of open fires and enjoy our secluded
garden. Cruelty-free, environment-friendly and organic products
used where possible.
G CatB V Ve NS Acc5

Shepherd's Purse ☎ 01947 820228, fax 01947 601670
95 Church Street, Whitby, North Yorkshire YO22 4BH
See display ad on page 43.
G CatB L V Ve NS Acc20

Dairy Guest House ☎ 01904 639367
3 Scarcroft Road, York YO2 1ND
Beautifully appointed Victorian town house, that was once the
local Dairy! Well equipped cottage-style rooms around a flower-
filled courtyard. Some en-suite. One four-poster. Listed as
Commended by the English Tourist Board. Informal atmosphere.
Non-smoking. Offers traditional or vegetarian B&B from £17 pp.
Please phone for colour brochure.
G CatB DA Ve NS Acc10

• *Cafés, restaurants, pubs*

Bharat Restaurant ☎ 01274 521200
502 Great Horton Road, Bradford, West Yorkshire BD7 3HR   R L a
South Square Vegetarian Café ☎ 01274 834928
South Square, Thornton Road, Thornton, Bradford, West Yorkshire
BD13 3LD   R/C c w NS
Brook's Restaurant ☎ 01484 715284
6 Bradford Road, Brighouse, West Yorkshire HD6 1RW   R L a pNS
Malt Shovel Inn ☎ 01423 862929
Brearton, Harrogate, North Yorkshire HG3 3BX   P L a
Tea Tree ☎ 01969 667817
Outhwaite House, Main Street, Hawes, North Yorkshire DL8 3QL
Small friendly vegetarian/wholefood teashop. Home baking. Good
coffee, light lunches, afternoon teas. Local crafts, candles, prints, old
books upstairs.   C c w NS
Pollyanna's Tearoom ☎ 01423 869208
Jockey Lane, Knaresborough, North Yorkshire HG3 0HF   C a NS
Fatty Arbuckles American Diner ☎ 0113 244 9016
Unit 13, Crown Point Retail Park, Junction Street, Leeds LS10 1ET
                                                               R L a pNS
Strawberry Fields Bistro & Wine Bar ☎ 0113 243 1515
159 Woodhouse Lane, Leeds LS2 3ED   R/Wine bar L a NS
The Curlew Café ☎ 01943 464351
11/13 Crossgate, Otley, West Yorkshire LS21 1AA   C c pNS
Herbs Restaurant ☎ 01756 790619
Above Healthy Life Natural Food Centre, 10 High Street, Skipton,
North Yorkshire BD23 1JZ   R c w NS
Bettys Café Tea Rooms ☎ 01904 659142
6-8 St Helens Square, York YO1 2QP   R/C L a pNS
Millers Yard Café ☎ 01904 610676
Millers Yard, Gillygate, York YO3 7EB   C c w NS
The Rubicon ☎ 01904 676076
5 Little Stonegate, York YO1 2AX
Bring your own wine, no charge. Best vegetarian food, large portions.
£6 2 course lunch, £12.50 3 course dinner, including juice and coffee.
                                                                 R c NS

North West England

Cheshire

• *Cafés, restaurants, pubs*

Fatty Arbuckles American Diner ☎ 01244 318129
  Unit 6, 6-13 Frodsham Street, Chester CH1 3JJ   R L a pNS
Fatty Arbuckles American Diner ☎ 0161 480 6763
  Grand Central, 18 Wellington Road South, Stockport SK1 3TA
                                                        R L a pNS

Cumbria

Rothay Manor   ☎ 015394 33605
Rothay Bridge, Ambleside LA22 0EH

Situated in the heart of the Lake District, this Regency country-house hotel (run by the Nixon family for over 25 years) has an international reputation for cuisine, comfort and relaxed atmosphere.
H CatA L Ve pNS Acc34

Lancrigg Vegetarian Country House Hotel   ☎ 015394 35317
Easedale Road, Grasmere LA22 9QN

Idyllic peaceful mountain setting in heart of English Lake District. Half a mile from Grasmere village. Historic house, much loved by Lakes poets and artists. Four-posters, and whirlpool baths. Thirty acres private grounds. Delicious vegetarian cuisine. Licensed.
H CatA L DA V Ve pNS CN Acc30

Chestnut House   ☎ 017683 71230
Crosby Garrett, Kirkby Stephen CA17 4PR

Delightful cottage in small village. Lovely walks from doorstep or ideal for touring Lakes and Yorkshire Dales. Two double/twin rooms with h & c. Delicious freshly made vegetarian/vegan breakfasts and evening meals; home-made bread, some vegetables home-grown.
G CatC V Ve NS CN Acc5

The Thrang   ☎ 017683 71889
Mallerstang, Kirkby Stephen CA17 4JX

Victorian vicarage in peaceful fell-side setting, between the Lakes and Dales. A perfect place for walking or just relaxing. Good Aga-cooked food. RAC "Highly Acclaimed". Phone for brochure – or e-mail j.hamilton@argonet.co.uk
H CatA L Ve pNS CN Acc11

Fair Place Wholefood Guest House
☎ 017684 86235, fax 017684 86066
Watermillock-on-Ullswater, Penrith CA11 0LR

We are 200 yards past Watermillock Church in a rural position. We welcome walkers, children and well-behaved pets. Our comfortable en-suite bedrooms have tea makers and electric fires, C.H. and colour TV. Drying facilities; off the road parking; marvellous facilities for listening to music. Vegetarian meals available one mile.
G CatB V Ve NS CN Acc4+2 children

• *Cafés, restaurants, pubs*

Stefan's Café-Bistro ☎ 015394 43535
Queen's Square, Bowness on Windermere LA23 3BY
Enjoy delicious English and Continental dishes freshly cooked and presented in our individual style. Varied menu appealing to all tastes.
R/C L a NS

Quince & Medlar ☎ 01900 823579
 11/13 Castlegate, Cockermouth CA13 9EU   R L c NS

A Room With A View ☎ 015394 36751
 1st Floor, Laburnum House, The Square, Hawkshead, Ambleside
 LA22 0LF   R L c NS

Lakeland Natural Waterside Café Restaurant and Shop
 ☎ 01539 729743
 Kent View, Waterside, Kendal LA9 4DZ
 Morning coffee, lunch, afternoon tea. Delicious home-made dishes served in a relaxed, welcoming atmosphere. Menu changes daily.
 Seats by river.   R/C c w NS

The Union Jack ☎ 01539 722458
 15 Kirkland, Kendal LA9 4AF   C L a pNS

The Old Forge Bistro ☎ 017683 71832
 39 North Road, Kirkby Stephen CA17 4RE   R/C L a w pNS

The Village Bakery ☎ 01768 881515, fax 01768 881848
 Melmerby, Penrith CA10 1HE
 See display ad above.   R a w NS

46

Little Salkeld Watermill ☎ 01768 881523
Little Salkeld, Penrith CA10 1NN
Tearoom and shop adjoining working traditional watermill producing organic stoneground flours. Tearoom produces home-baked food from fresh flour and range of fresh local produce. Open Monday, Tuesday, Thursday, March-October. C b w NS

Isle of Man

Fernleigh   ☎ 01624 842435
Marine Parade, Peel IM5 1PB

Looking across the bay, in the quiet fishing town of Peel. Offering home-made traditional and imaginative vegetarian fare, with choice of menu for breakfast and dinner, freshly prepared to your order daily. Standard and en-suite rooms. 2 Crown Commended. H CatB Ve pNS Acc22

Prospect Cottage (see page48)

Prospect Cottage   ☎ 015242 41328

Bank End, Ingleton, via Carnforth, Lancashire LA6 3HE

Vegetarian/vegan B&B, tranquility and a warm welcome at Lauraine's picturesque home in Ingleton village, centre for Yorkshire Dales and close to South Lakeland. Fells, caves, waterfalls and limestone scenery of breathtaking beauty. *Although mail goes via Carnforth in Lancashire, Ingleton is in North Yorkshire.*
PH CatC V Ve NS Acc3/4

• *Cafés, restaurants, pubs*

Fatty Arbuckles American Diner   ☎ 01253 291642
    89-93 Church Street, Blackpool FY3 8JG   R L a pNS

Lennard Eating House   ☎ 01253 28167
    8 Deansgate, Blackpool FY1 1BN   C a pNS

Libra Vegetarian Restaurant   ☎ 01524 61551
    19 Brock Street, Lancaster LA1 1UR   R/C c w NS

Everyman Bistro   ☎ 0151 708 9545
    5-9 Hope Street, Liverpool L1 9BH
    'This counter service restaurant has a reputation for well priced, freshly prepared, wholesome food. The menu offers a wide range of vegetarian dishes.' *BBC Vegetarian Good Food*   R/C L a w pNS

Fatty Arbuckles American Diner   ☎ 0151 221 0559
    Montrose Way, Edge Lane Retail Park, Liverpool L13 3EW   R L a pNS

The Greenbank Restaurant   ☎ 0151 734 4498
    332 Smithdown Road, Liverpool L15   R L a pNS

Café Pop   ☎ 0161 237 9688
    34-36 Oldham Street, Manchester M1 1JN
    A bizarre combination of gorgeous vegetarian dishes in a go's coffee bar setting – Britain's only 'slow food' café.   C c pNS

Misty's Vegetarian Café   ☎ 0161 256 3355
    Unit 3, Longsight Shopping Centre, 531 Stockport Road, Longsight, Manchester M12 4JH   C c

'On The Eighth Day' Co-op. Ltd. ☎ 0161 273 1850
107-109 Oxford Road, All Saints, Manchester M1 7DU
Manchester's longest established vegetarian restaurant. Fresh food
prepared daily. Friendly, smoke-free environment. International,
award-winning menu changes daily. Open 10am-7pm Monday -
Saturday.   C c NS

Sunflower Vegan Restaurant ☎ 0161 236 9805
Tommy Duck's Pub, 111 Newton Street, Manchester City Centre
                                                                         R L d w

Woody's ☎ 01457 871197
5 King Street, Delph, Oldham OL3 5DL   R L c NS

The Salcombe lifeboat puts to sea.

Wales

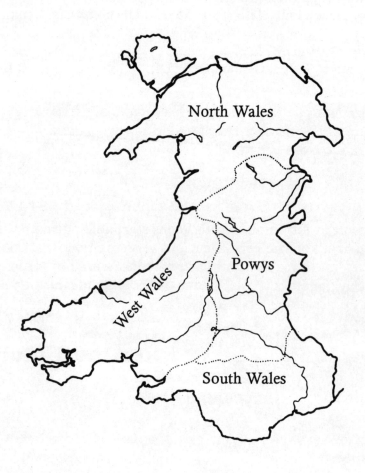

North Wales

Powys

West Wales

South Wales

North Wales

Bwthyn
☎ 01248 713119

Brynafon, Menai Bridge, Isle of Anglesey LL59 5HA

Warm, welcoming, non-smoking B&B, £15.00 p.p. (double), in pretty Victorian terrace a minute from the Menai Straits and Telford's elegant suspension bridge, 1 mile A5/A55, 40 minutes Holyhead ferry. Two beautifully-fitted en-suite doubles, each with colour TV, tea/coffee makers, power shower etc. Delicious traditional/vegetarian breakfast, dinner optional. Special 3-day break for over 45s – DB&B £79 p.p. WTB 2 Crown Highly Commended Award. Come as guests – leave as friends. NB If telephone number changes, operator will advise.
PH CatC Ve NS Acc4

Clwt Cotal Helygen
☎ 01341 247580

Glan y Wern, Dyffryn Ardudwy, Gwynedd LL44 2EP

A welcome awaits in our North Wales smallholding and pottery (5 miles south of Harlech). Delicious vegetarian meals are our speciality, much made with organic produce from our garden – and lovely puddings! Please phone either John or Linda for further information.
G CatC V Ve NS Acc8

Snowdonia: The Old Rectory Hotel
☎ 01766 590305

Maentwrog, nr Blaenau Ffestiniog, Gwynedd LL41 4HN

Hotel and licensed restaurant, amidst a three acre riverside garden. Near Portmeirion/Harlech. Informal atmosphere. Main house and budget annex, all en-suite. Italian and vegetarian/vegan menus. Family and 3+ nights discounts.
H CatB L Ve pNS CN Acc24

Tremeifion Vegetarian Country Hotel

☎ 01766 770491

Soar Road, Talsarnau, nr Harlech, Gwynedd LL47 6UH

See display ad below.
H CatB V Ve NS CN Acc10

Rawcliffe Guest House   ☎ 01978 266451

3 Belmont Road, Wrexham LL13 7PW

Friendly B&B, £15 p.n., offering good food and comfortable accommodation. Vegetarian and traditional meals. Guests' TV lounge, separate dining room, car parking facilities. Ideal touring/walking base for North Wales, 11 miles from Chester. Special winter breaks. No pets. Phone for brochure.
G CatC NS Acc6

- *Cafés, restaurants, pubs*

Chandlers Brasserie ☎ 01492 640991
  Trefriw, Conwy LL27 0JH   R L a NS
Fatty Arbuckles American Diner ☎ 01745 344422
  Childrens Village, The Promenade, Kinmel Bay, Rhyl, Wrexham
  LL18 5ED   R L a pNS

Powys

The Old Post Office   ☎ 01497 820008
Llanigon, Hay-on-Wye, via Hereford HR3 5QA

A very special find at the foot of the Black Mountains
and only two miles from the famous second-
hand book town of Hay-on-Wye.
Charming 17th century house with
beams and oak floor boards. Lovely
walks and views of Wye Valley and
Black Mountains. Dogs by
arrangement.
G CatB V Ve NS CN Acc6

- *Cafés, restaurants, pubs*

Cain Valley Hotel ☎ 01691 648366
  High Street, Llanfyllin SY22 5AQ   R L a w pNS
The Old Station Coffee Shop ☎ 01650 531338
  Dinas Mawddwy, Machynlleth SY20 9LS
  Set amongst mountains at top of Dovey Valley, 1 mile north of A470
  junction with A458 from Welshpool. At entrance to Meirion Mill.
                                              R L a w NS
Carole's Cake Shop & Old Swan Tearooms ☎ 01597 811060
  West Street, Rhayader LD6 5AB
  Seventeenth-century tearooms, situated in the lakeland of Wales.
  Serving home-made meals, salads and freshly baked home-made cakes
  and sweets.   C a NS

South Wales

Dafs Guesthouse

☎ and fax 01792 475731

116 Bryn Road, Brynmill, Swansea, Glamorgan SA2 0AT

E-mail afswales@cix.compulink.co.uk

Experience the culture and history of Wales in the city that is the gateway to the Gower, with its castles, golden beaches, spectacular coastal cliffs and wild moorland ponies. Exotic international cuisine - optional evening meal £7.50. Multilingual hostess also offers English conversation classes.

PH CatC Ve NS Acc6

The West Usk Lighthouse

☎ 01633 810126/815582

St Brides, Wentloog, nr Newport, Gwent NP1 9SF

Stay in a real 170 year old lighthouse, situated between Newport and Cardiff. Grade II listed, with rooms wedge-shaped and furnished with a waterbed, four-poster bed and flotation tank. Great for couples, singles and children. Peaceful, relaxing and different. All amenities nearby.

G CatA Ve NS CN Acc10

Oldcastle Court (see opposite page).

Oldcastle Court

☎ 01873 890285

Pandy, Abergavenny, Monmouthshire NP7 7PH

Beautiful thirteenth-century farmhouse, with oak beams and oak staircase, built on castle site near Black Mountains, Offa's Dyke Path and Hay-on-Wye, oldest town in Wales. Great base for walking or pony trekking (available nearby). Please phone for brochure.
PH CatC CN Acc6

• *Cafés, restaurants, pubs*

Fatty Arbuckles American Diner ☎ 01222 233671
  50 St Mary Street, Cardiff CF1 1SP   R L a pNS
Fatty Arbuckles American Diner ☎ 01633 277980
  Newport Retail Park, Spytty Road, Newport, Gwent NP9 0QQ
                                                        R L a pNS

West Wales

Grove Park Guest House

☎ 01239 820122

Pen-y-Bont, Newport, Pembrokeshire SA42 0LT

Secluded small and friendly house on the edge of coastal town and at the foot of Preseli hills. Spectacular views. No smoking. Bird Sanctuary and Pembrokeshire coastal path 100 yards. Pony trekking, sailing nearby. Fishguard 7 miles, Cardigan 12 miles. Vegetarians welcome.
G CatB L Ve NS Acc8

Warpool Court Hotel

☎ 01437 720300, fax 01437 720676

St David's, Pembrokeshire SA62 6BN

This 25-bedroom, privately owned hotel is set in seven acres with panoramic sea views. All dishes are individually prepared and all tastes catered for. A separate vegetarian menu is always available. Food awards include a merit from the RAC and 2 rosettes from the AA.
H CatA L DA Ve pNS Acc56

The Old Court House Vegetarian Guest House

☎ 01348 837095

Trefin, nr St Davids, Pembrokeshire SA62 5AX

A warm welcome awaits you at our 150-year old cottage, just five minutes' walk from the Pembrokeshire coastal path, offering en-

suite accommodation, an open fire and delicious vegetarian/ vegan food. Self-guided walking holidays and climbing activities are also available.

G CatB V Ve NS Acc6

Scotland

Orkney and Shetland
Islands (NE of the
Scottish mainland,
here shown at half
scale of main map)

Scottish Highlands

Western Scottish
Islands

Aberdeenshire
and Moray

Angus, Perth and
Kinross

Argyll

Fife

Central
Scotland

Lothian

Ayrshire

Borders

Dumfries and
Galloway

Aberdeenshire and Moray

Inverdeen House B&B

☎ 013397 55759

Bridge Square, Ballater, Royal Deeside, Aberdeenshire AB35 5QJ

100% non-smoking. Helpful, adaptable, experienced regarding dietary and environmental special needs. Outstanding food using fresh ingredients ... consult when booking. Comfortable 1820 listed building. Period ambience. Excellent beds, amenities, central heating. Highland scenery. French, German, Polish spoken. Send for brochure.
PH CatC Ve NS Acc6

Gordon Arms Hotel

☎ 013398 84236, fax 013398 84401

Kincardine O'Neil, Royal Deeside, Aberdeenshire AB34 5AA

Small family-run Victorian hotel in oldest village on Royal Deeside. Comfortable en-suite rooms, log fires and period antiques. 20% of our menus are vegetarian - all home cooking. Centrally positioned for touring and all the local attractions. STB 3 Crowns.
H CatB L Ve CN Acc20

Minton House

☎ 01309 690819, fax 01309 691583

Findhorn, Moray IV36 0YY

Standing on the shore of Findhorn Bay in an area blessed with clear light and natural beauty, Minton is a haven of peace, rest and healing. Retreats, workshops, meditation sanctuary, sauna, hot tub, library, massage, home cooking and a friendly welcome.
G CatB DA V Ve NS CN Acc20

Angus and Perth & Kinross

• *Cafés, restaurants, pubs*

Fatty Arbuckles American Diner ☎ 01382 624198
Stacks Leisure Park, Harefield Road, Dundee DD2 3XN

R L a pNS

Ayrshire

• *Cafés, restaurants, pubs*

Hopkins Coffee House ☎ 01292 318750
9C Church Street, Troon KA10 6AU

C a w NS

Borders

• *Cafés, restuarants, pubs*

Tibbie Shiel's Inn ☎ 01750 42231
St Mary's Loch, Selkirkshire TD7 5NE

R/P L a pNS

Dumfries and Galloway

• *Cafés, restaurants, pubs*

Abbey Cottage Coffees and Crafts ☎ 01387 850377
26 Main Street, New Abbey, Dumfries DG2 8BY

R L a NS

Opus Salad Bar ☎ 01387 255752
95 Queensberry Street, Dumfries DG1 1BH

C L a pNS

Edinburgh and Lothian

Six Mary's Place Guest House

☎ 0131 332 8965

Raeburn Place, Edinburgh EH4 1JD

http://ourworld.compuserve.com/homepages/ECT_Social_Firm
s/smp1

Beautifully restored Georgian townhouse with STB Two Crown Commended status, specialising in vegetarian cuisine and offering a smoke-free environment. Delightful conservatory and restful gardens. Contact Elaine Gale.

G CatA V Ve NS Acc13

Studio Bed & Breakfast   ☎ 0131 662 9768

39 Gilmour Road, Edinburgh EH16 5NS

A friendly welcome in informal vegetarian home in quiet residential area well served by buses. Central heating, good food, tasteful decor in Edwardian house. Contact Sue Lieberman.

PH CatB V Ve NS Acc2

- *Cafés, restaurants, pubs*

Helios Fountain ☎ 0131 229 7884
   7 Grassmarket, Edinburgh EH1 2HY
   A friendly vegetarian coffee house selling tasty food ranging from the wholesome to the positively wicked. Also an unusual shop.   C c NS

Henderson's Salad Table ☎ 0131 225 2131
   94 Hanover Street, Edinburgh EH2 1DR   R/C L c w pNS

Isabel's Café ☎ 0131 662 4014
   83 Clerk Street, Edinburgh EH8 9JG   C c NS

Kalpna Restaurant ☎ 0131 667 9890
   2/3 St Patrick Square, Edinburgh EH8 9EZ   R L c NS

Parrots ☎ 0131 229 3252
   3 Viewforth, Edinburgh EH10 4JD   R L a NS

Fife

• Cafés, restaurants, pubs

Sunflowers ☎ 01592 646266
39 Whytescauseway, Kirkcaldy KY1 1XY
Vegetarian specialities – homebaking, soups, toasties, baked potatoes.
Calorie-counted meals, snacks and cakes. Freshly ground coffee, fine
wines and beers. R L c w NS

Glasgow and Central Scotland

• Cafés, restaurants, pubs

Fatty Arbuckles American Diner ☎ 0141 941 2017
23 Britannia Way, Clydebank Retail Shopping Centre, Clydebank,
Dunbartonshire G81 2RZ R L a pNS
Fatty Arbuckles American Diner ☎ 0141 332 3640
196 Hope Street, Glasgow G2 2UE R L a pNS

Ladyfinger ☎ 0141 353 0777
7 Buccleuch Street, off Cambridge Street, Glasgow
See display ad on page 61.

The Scottish Highlands

The Pines Country House ☎ 01479 841220
Duthil, Carr-Bridge, Inverness-shire PH23 3ND

STB 3 Crowns Commended. Relax and enjoy our Highland hospitality. Set in mature woodlands where nature comes alive: red squirrels, birds, rabbits. Personal service, clean and comfortable en-suite rooms with tea/coffee making, TV, radio. Walking, birdwatching, golf, skiing and lots more. Children and pets welcomed. Open all year.
G CatB Ve pNS CN Acc6

Rhu Mhor Guest House ☎ 01397 702213
Alma Road, Fort William, Inverness-shire PH33 6BP

A traditional guest house set in a steep acre of secluded wild garden, but only ten minutes walk from bus and train stations. Car parking. Home-cooked vegetarian and vegan meals  by arrangement. Telephone for brochure.
G CatB Ve pNS Acc15

Cuildorag House
☎ 01855 821529

Onich, nr Fort William, Inverness-shire PH33 6SD

Friendly welcome, comfortable Victorian house, big breakfast. Spectacular lochs and mountains. Ideal centre for hill walking, touring, exploring Ben Nevis, Glencoe, Loch Ness, islands Mull and Skye a short drive away. Steam trains, castles, mountain biking, wildlife, skiing ...
PH CatC V VE NS Acc6

Culag (Julie & Brian Neath)
☎ 01599 555341

Carr Brae, Dornie, Kyle of Lochalsh, Ross-shire IV40 8HA

Peaceful secluded woodland setting overlooking Loch Duich, with spectacular views of mountains and sea. Ideal centre for exploring Kintail, Glenelg, Plockton and Skye. Excellent area for hillwalkers and naturalists. En-suite available. B&B from £15, EM £9. Exclusively vegetarian/vegan.
PH CatC V Ve NS CN Acc4

Taigh Na Mara Vegetarian Guesthouse
☎ 01854 655282, fax 01854 655292

The Shore, Ardindrean, Lochbroom, nr Ullapool, Wester Ross IV23 2SE

From their idyllic and secluded lochside home Tony and Jackie offer gourmet Scottish vegan cooking, vegetarian information, their notorious cookbook *Rainbows & Wellies* (£14.95), their guide *Scotland the Green* (£4.95), and the key to unlock the dreams and wonder of the Highlands.
G CatB Vegan NS CN Acc6

The Ceilidh Place
☎ 01854 612103

West Argyle Street, Ullapool, Ross & Cromarty IV26 2TY

The Ceilidh Place is a complex of old buildings offering both posh rooms and bunk rooms. All day food, art gallery, bookshop and a wonderful programme of events combine to make The Ceilidh Place unique. Now in its 27th year!
H & Bunkhouse CatA & CatB L Ve pNS Acc44

Sumundar Villa
☎ and fax 01408 621717

Harbour Road, Brora, Sutherland KW9 6QF

Comfortable family home at the mouth of River Brora, looking onto the North Sea. A little corner of heaven. Seals, otters, dolphins, fossil beach. Miles of golden sands. One hour from John O'Groats and Orkney ferry. Good home cooking.
PH CatB DA Ve NS Acc8+cot

Invercassley Cottage
☎ 01549 441288

Rosehall, by Lairg, Sutherland IV27 4BD

For good food, good music, good company come to Invercassley Cottage, set in its wild and organic garden overlooking Strathoykel. Stay the night or longer, use our canoes or bikes to explore the beautiful rivers, mountains and glens just on the doorstep. Campers welcome. Garden chalet avaliable.
PH CatC Ve pNS CN Acc7

• Cafés, restaurants, pubs

Dunnet Head Tearoom ☎ 01847 851774
Brough, by Thurso, Caithness KW14 8YE   C a NS

The River Café & Restaurant ☎ 01463 714884
10 Bank Street, Inverness IV1 1QY
Attractive riverside coffee shop and restaurant. Our menu changes daily and includes a selection of fresh vegetarian dishes.
                                                            R/C L a w NS

Station Tea Room and Craft Shop ☎ 01349 865894
Station Square, Dingwall, Ross-shire IV15 9JD   C a NS

Seafood Restaurant ☎ 01599 534813
Railway Buildings, Kyle of Lochalsh, Wester Ross   R L a NS

Seagreen Restaurant & Bookshop ☎ 01599 534388
Plockton Road, Kyle of Lochalsh, Wester Ross IV40 8DA
Food all cooked on premises. All day licensed café. Garden. Wholefood shop. Outside terrace. Exhibition space. Traditional music. Local interest literature.
                                                            R/C L a w NS

Shetland Islands

Bayanne House
☎ 01957 744219

Sellafirth, Yell ZE2 9DG

Traditional merchant's house on beach at Basta Voe. Ideally situated for bird and otter watching. We grow our own produce organically on our croft, which is designated an environmentally sensitive area.

Breakfast: homemade bread, muesli, yoghurt.

Dinner: soufflés/quiches with our own eggs and milk, wild mushrooms, fresh vegetables.

PH CatC Ve NS Acc3

The Western Scottish Islands

Mrs Lena MacLennan ☎ 01859 550285
1 Horgabost, Isle of Harris, Western Isles HS3 3HR
See display ad on page 65.
PH CatB CN Acc6

Argyll Hotel ☎ 01681 700334, fax 01681 700510
Isle of Iona, Argyll PA76 6SJ
Friendly hotel on the seashore in the village of Iona. Cosy lounges with open fires, plant-filled sunlounge, spacious dining room with family portraits and antiques. Cottagey bedrooms with original paintings, nearly all have en-suite facilities. Real home cooking using local produce and our organic vegetables in season. We always have a fresh vegetarian choice. Residents' and table licence.
H CatA L Ve pNS Acc26

Iona Cottage ☎ 01681 700579
Isle of Iona, Argyll PA76 6SJ
Iona Cottage is a 200 year old croft house which stands on a rise facing the jetty. Come and enjoy fresh air, home cooking and an open fire on this sacred island. Packed lunches, guided walks and winter retreats also available.
G CatB V Ve NS Acc6

The Willows ☎ 01851 621321
Deb & David Nash, 19 Tolsta Chaolais, Isle of Lewis, Western Isles HS2 9DW
Set in a very beautiful lochside location, our island crofthouse is the perfect setting for those seeking peace, wildlife, marine/bird life, magnificent sandy beaches, history: 3 miles from Callanish Stones, Scotland's Stonehenge. We're renowned for wonderful vegetarian/vegan cookery (evening meal optional) and cater for every meatless diet. We offer a twin bedroom, private sitting and

bathroom, a real welcome and a stay you'll never forget.
PH CatC DA V Ve pNS CN Acc2

Bruach Mhor ☎ 01681 700276
Fionnphort, Isle of Mull, Argyll PA66 6BL

Comfortable, centrally heated croft house, half-mile from Iona ferry. Home cooking, including varied vegetarian menu. Enjoy the Ross of Mull's splendid scenery, seascapes, wildlife, geology. Walkers welcome. Packed lunches available.
PH CatC Ve pNS Acc6

Sunset behind the islands off the western Scottish coast.

Donmar
☎ 01470 532204

43 Bernisdale, Isle of Skye, Inverness-shire IV51 9NS

Traditional croft house surrounded by open countryside, 7 miles from Portree, 15 miles from Dunvegan. Views of Storr and Cuillin mountains. Optional evening meal. Reductions for children. Pets welcome. En-suite. Riding, boat trips, golf etc. nearby.
PH CatB Ve pNS CN Acc6

Langdale House
☎ 01471 822376

Waterloo, Breakish, Isle of Skye, Inverness-shire IV42 8QE

Langdale House has breathtaking views of sea and hills of Skye and Wester Ross. Sea and land birds, Atlantic and common seals on view from lounge. A true wildlife experience. All bedrooms are en-suite and have TV and satelite. Licensed. Dinner available.
PH CatB Ve pNS CN Acc6

The Tables Hotel
☎ and fax 01470 521404

Dunvegan, Isle of Skye, Inverness-shire IV55 8WA

A small and friendly hotel centrally situated in Dunvegan village (castle 3/4 mile), overlooking Loch Dunvegan, with a relaxed informal atmosphere, imaginative home cooking, residents' and table licence. An ideal touring or walking base for North Skye.
H CatB L Ve pNS Acc10

Further vegetarian information

For users of this guide who would like further information on vegetarianism or veganism in Britain, or information on a particular area, we list below a number of organisations, groups and information centres.

National

Friends Vegetarian Society
   9 Astons Close, Woods Lane, Amblecote, nr Stourbridge, West Midlands DY5 2QT, tel 01383 423899
Jewish Vegetarian Society
   855 Finchley Road, London NW11 8LX, tel 0181 455 0692
The Vegetarian Society (UK) Ltd.
   Parkdale, Dunham Road, Altrincham, Cheshire WA14 4QG, tel 0161 928 0793, fax 0161 926 9182
The Vegan Society Ltd.
   7 Battle Road, St Leonards-on-Sea, East Sussex TN37 7AA, tel 01424 427393, fax 01424 717064

England (by county)

South Bedfordshire Vegetarian Group
   61 Church Street, Leighton Buzzard, Bedfordshire LU7 7BT, tel 01525 852443
Reading Vegetarian & Food Reform Society
   161 Westwood Road, Tilehurst, Reading, Berkshire RG3 6LP, tel 01734 421619
Milton Keynes & District Vegetarians
   13 Peers Lane, Shenley Church End, Milton Keynes, Buckinghamshire MK5 6BG, tel 01908 503919
South Bucks Vegetarians
   121 Deeds Grove, High Wycombe, Buckinghamshire HP12 3NY, tel 01494 440946
Cambridge Vegetarians
   13 Emery Street, Cambridge CB1 2AX, tel 01223 69544
Somersham Vegetarian Information Centre
   45 The Trundle, Somersham, Huntingdon, Cambridgeshire PE17 3JS, tel 01487 740251

Chester & Clwyd Vegetarians
Nant Yr Hafod Cottage, Hafod Bilston, Llandegla LL11 3BG, tel 01978 790442

Halton Information Centre
17 Norton View, Halton Village, Runcorn, Cheshire WA7 2PB, tel 01928 580175

Holmes Chapel Information Centre
16 Elm Drive, Holmes Chapel, Cheshire CW4 7QG, tel 01477 544574

South Cheshire Vegetarian Group
17 Springfield Drive, Crewe CW2 6RA, tel 01270 69238

Cleveland Information Centre
6 Thropton Close, Billingham, Cleveland TS23 2TQ, tel 01642 563730

North Cornwall Vegetarian Information Centre
Hilltop Animal Haven, Thurdon, Kilkhampton, Bude, Cornwall EX23 9RZ, tel 01288 321268

Right Life Information Centre
49 Upper Chapel, Launceston, Cornwall PL15 7DW, tel 01566 776256

Kendal Vegetarians
Low House, New Hutton, Kendal, Cumbria LA8 0AZ, tel 01539 725219

Lakes Vegetarians
19 Loughrigg Park, Ambleside, Cumbria LA22 0DY, tel 015394 33901

Castle Donington Vegetarian Information Centre
Sunflower Cottage, Bondgate, Castle Donington, Derby DE7 2NR, tel 01332 810946

Derbyshire Vegetarian Information Centre
42 Hawthorn Crescent, Findern, Derby DE65 6AN, tel 01283 703059

Marple/New Mills Information Centre
9 Kinder View, New Mills, Derbyshire SK12 4DB, tel 01663 742102

Clovelly & District Information Centre
South View, Woolsery, Bideford, North Devon EX39 5QP, tel 01237 431074

South Hams Information Centre
Flat 7B, Glenelg House, Dyncombe Street, Kingsbridge, South Devon TQ7 1LR, tel 01548 856768

Bournemouth Vegetarian Society
6 Hayes Avenue, Bournemouth, Dorset, tel 01202 391836

Poole Information Centre
  245 Hasler Road, Canford Heath, Poole, Dorset BH17 9AH, tel 01202 691952
Colchester Vegetarian Society
  P.O. Box 3236, Colchester, Essex CO6 4LW, tel 01206 263545
Forest Vegetarian Group
  9 Russell Road, Buckhurst Hill, Essex IG9 5QJ
Mid Essex Vegetarians
  The Little House, Hall Road, Panfield, Braintree, Essex CM7 5AW, tel 01376 324559
Southend Area Veggies Information Centre
  59 Stambridge Road, Rochford, Essex SS4 1DY, tel 01702 540903
Cheltenham Vegetarians
  30 High Street, Cheltenham, Gloucestershire GL50 1DZ, tel 01242 232776
Kathleen Keleney-Williams, Information Centre
  Coombe Lodge Flat, Wotton under Edge, Gloucestershire GL12 7NB, tel 01453 843165
NEMSEL Vegetarian Group
  12 Gwendor Avenue, Crumpsall, Manchester M8 4LE, tel 0161 740 5917
N.W. Manchester Vegetarian Information Centre
  31 Riding Fold Lane, Worsley, Manchester M28 2UR, tel 0161 728 2061
Petersfield/East Hampshire Vegetarian Information Centre
  2 Hazel Road, Clanfield, Hampshire PO8 0LF, tel 01705 592152
Portsmouth Area Vegetarian Network
  38 Meredith Road, Hilsea, Portsmouth PO2 9NN, tel 01705 667420
Solent Vegetarians & Vegans
  70 Stuart Crescent, Stanmore, Winchester, Hampshire SO22 4AS, tel 01962 867648
North London & Barnet Vegetarian Group
  12 Doggetts Court, East Barnet, Hertfordshire EN4 8SJ, 0181 441 1880
Letchworth & District Vegetarian Society
  Wilbury Hill Farm House, Wilbury Hills Road, Letchworth, Hertfordshire SG6 4LB, tel 01462 485128
The Haven Vegetarian Information Centre
  1 South Hill Road, Hemel Hempstead, Hertfordshire HP1 1JB, tel 01442 257220

Isle of Wight Vegetarians
  Leaholme, Appley Road, Ryde, Isle of Wight PO33 1NE, tel 01983
  568984
Vectis Vegetarians
  3 Alvington Close, Carisbrooke, Newport, Isle of Wight PO30 5AS,
  tel 01983 529353
BEVEG
  P.O. Box 317, Beckenham, Kent BR3 1WP
Canterbury & District Information Centre
  83 Cherry Gardens, Herne Bay, Kent CT6 5QY, tel 01227 375661
Northfleet Vegetarian Information Centre
  Basement Flat, 48c Hamerton Road, Northfleet, Kent DA11 9DX, tel
  01474 536523
Orpington Information Centre
  162a Orpington High Street, Orpington, Kent BR6 0JR, 01689
  875797
Cleveleys Vegetarian Information Centre
  4 Sherwood Place, Anchorsholme, Cleveleys, Lancashire FY5 3BS, tel
  01253 827411
Preston Vegetarian & Vegan Group
  68 Howick Park Drive, Penwortham, Preston, Lancashire PR1 0LX,
  tel 01772 744743
Leicester Information Centre
  Rectory Field Nursery, Wanlip, Leicester LE7 4PL, tel 0116 267 4613
Boston Vegetarian Group
  The Shrubbery, Station Road, Old Leeke, Lincolnshire PE22 9RF, tel
  01205 871152
Gainsborough Vegetarians
  9 Gainas Avenue, Gainsborough, Lincolnshire DN21 2RA, tel 01427
  612149
Louth Vegetarian Information Centre
  Hope Cottage, Bond Hayes Lane, Hagworthington, nr Spilsby,
  Lincolnshire PE23 4LQ, tel 01507 588661
'Voice of Lincolnshire' Information Centre
  Myrtle Cottage, 31 Main Street, North Kyme, Lincoln LN4 4DF, tel
  01526 861426
Greenwich Information Centre
  58 Eaglesfield Road, Shooters Hill, London SE18 3BU, tel 0181 317 1424

London Vegans
7 Deansbrook Road, Edgeware, Middlesex HA8 9BE
Liverpool Vegetarian Information Centre
tel 0151 489 4273
Merseyside Vegetarian Helplink
38 Hyacinth Close, Haydock, St Helens, Merseyside WA11 0NZ, tel
01942 271761
Southport & District Information Centre
c/o 44 Shaws Road, Birkdale, Southport, Merseyside PR8 4LP, tel
01704 562378
Harrow Vegetarian Group
59 Stuart Avenue, South Harrow, Middlesex HA2 9AS, tel 0181 869 1152
Norfolk & Norwich Vegetarian Society
4 Woodland Drive, Kirby Cane, nr Bungay, Suffolk NR35 2PT, tel
01508 518686
Wellingborough Information Centre
8 Brampton Close, Wellingborough, Northamptonshire NN8 5XG, tel
01933 674311
Northumberland & Newcastle Information Centre
Shieldhall, Wallington, Morpeth, Northumberland NE61 4AQ, tel
01670 540387 (ask for Kerry)
Northumberland Vegetarian Society
100 Stanley Street South, Blyth, Northumberland NE24 3BX, tel
01670 367836
Nottingham Vegetarian & Vegan Society
180 Mansfield Road, Nottingham NG1 3HU, tel 0115 958 5666
Oxford Vegetarians
57 Sharland Close, Grove, Wantage, Oxfordshire OX12 0AF, tel
01235 769425
Shropshire Vegetarian Information Centre
Overdale, The Mines, Benthall, nr Broseley, Shropshire TF12 5QY, tel
01629 583797
Bristol Vegetarian Society
6 Oakridge Close, Sidcot, Winscombe BS25 1LY, tel 01934 843853
Downend Vegetarian Information Centre
66 Coronation Road, Downend, Bristol BS16 5SL, tel 0117 956 2017
Exmoor Vegetarian Information Centre
Exmoor Lodge, Chapel Street, Exford, Somerset TA24 7PY, tel 01643
831694

Somerset Vegetarian Group
17 Foxdown Terrace, Wellington, Somerset TA21 8BC, tel 01823 660747
Yeovil & District Vegetarian Contact Group
159 Preston Road, Yeovil, Somerset BA20 2EF, tel 01963 22970
Lichfield Vegetarian Information Centre
49 Grange Lane, Lichfield, Staffordshire WS13 7EE, tel 01543 415136
Lowestoft Information Centre
44 Florence Road, Pakefield, Lowestoft, Suffolk NR33 7BY, tel 01502 563246
Croydon Vegetarian Group
Flat 23, Zodiac Court, 165 London Road, Croydon, Surrey CR0 2RJ, tel 0181 688 6325
Guildford Vegetarians
20 Burnet Avenue, Guildford, Surrey GU1 1YD, tel 01483 69257
Kingston & Richmond Vegetarians
87 Porchester Road, Kingston-upon-Thames, Surrey KT1 3PW, tel 0181 541 3437
Lingfield Information Centre
Staff Flat, Claridge House, Dormans Road, Dormansland, Surrey RH7 6QH
Brighton Vegetarian & Vegan Group
14 Terminus Street, Brighton, Sussex BN1 3PE, tel 01273 203184
Bognor Regis & District Information Centre
Sunlea, 119 Middleton Road, Middleton on Sea, West Sussex PO22 6DA, tel 01243 587759
Hastings Vegetarians
Quarry Wood, 23 Grange Road, Hastings, East Sussex TN34 2RL, tel 01424 751119
Horsham Vegetarian Group
50 Manorfields, Roffey, Horsham, Sussex RH13 6SB, tel 01403 241950
Coast Vegetarian Group
34 Victoria Avenue, Whitley Bay, Tyne & Wear NE26 2AZ, tel 0191 251 0377
Coventry Vegetarians
8 Eden Croft, Kenilworth, Warwickshire CV8 2BG, tel 01926 854139
Stourbridge Vegetarian Group
31 Witton Street, Norton, Stourbridge, West Midlands DY8 3YF, tel 01384 441822

Salisbury & District Vegetarian Information Centre
  1 George Street, Salisbury, Wiltshire SP2 7BA, tel 01722 331542
Worcestershire & South Warwickshire Vegetarian Group
  The Cottage, 58 Lower Cladswell Lane, Cookhill, Alcester B49 5JY,
  tel 01527 893820
Beeston & Morley Vegetarian Information Centre
  131 Old Lane, Beeston, Leeds LS11 7AQ, tel 0113 270 1923
Bradford Vegetarian Society
  66 Kirkgate, Shipley, West Yorkshire BD18 3EL, tel 01274 598455
Hull Veggies
  29 Heslerton Avenue, Cottingham, nr Hull HU16 5HW, tel 01482
  844165
Kirklees Vegetarian Information Centre
  8 Elms Hill, Slaithwaite, Huddersfield HD7 5HR, tel 01484 842326
Leeds Vegetarian & Vegan Society
  41 Hillcourt Drive, Leeds LS13 2AN, tel 0113 257 2760
Sheffield & District Vegetarian Society
  2 Cavendish Terrace, West Handley, Sheffield S31 9RZ, tel 01246 433013
Sheffield Vegan Society
  c/o 6 Cherry Tree Court, Cherry Tree Road, Sheffield S11 9AB, tel
  0114 258 9689
Wakefield & Huddersfield Vegetarian Information Centre
  29 Carr Gate Mount, Wrenthorpe, Wakefield WF2 0QP, tel 01924
  823354
York Vegetarians
  43 Ashley Park Road, Stockton Lane, York YO3 0JX

Scotland

Aberdeen Vegetarian Information Centre
  17 Howburn Place, Aberdeen AB11 6XT, tel 01224 573034
Glasgow District Vegetarian Information Centre
  53 Blackthorn Avenue, Beith, Ayrshire KA15 2AR, tel 01505 502565
Inverness Veggies
  P.O. Box 1, Drumnadrochit, Inverness-shire IV3 6TU, tel 01456 450596
Middleton-Holm Information Centre
  Middleton, Holm, Orkney KW17 2SD, tel 01856 781467
Perth Vegetarians
  The Cross, Errol, Perth PH2 7QW, tel 01821 642684

Scottish Highlands Vegetarian Information Centre
  Taigh Na Mara, The Shore, Ardindrean, Lochbroom, nr Ullapool,
  Wester Ross IV23 2SE, tel 01854 655282
South East Scotland Vegetarians
  135 Comely Bank Road, Edinburgh EH4 1BH, tel 0131 332 3961
Stonehouse Vegetarian Information Centre
  Dunrigh, Queen Street, Stonehouse, Lanarkshire ML9 3EE, tel 01698
  791512
Upper Deeside Vegetarian Information Centre
  2 Dairy Cottages, Balmoral Estate, Crathie, Ballater, Aberdeenshire
  AB35 5TB

Wales

Cardiff Vegetarians
  24 Snowden Road, Ely, Cardiff CF5 4PR, tel 01222 593376
Colwyn Bay Information Centre
  1st Floor, 114 Conway Road, Colwyn Bay LL29 7LL, tel 01492
  532024
Gwynedd Information Centre
  4 Bryn Hedydd, Llanllechid, Bangor, Gwynedd LL57 3HR, tel 01248
  602532
Mid-Glamorgan Vegetarian Information Centre
  25A Castle Street, Maesteg, Mid Glamorgan CF34 9YH, tel 01656
  733685
Pontypridd Vegetarian Information Centre
  11 Oxford Street, Treforest, Pontypridd CF37 1RU, tel 01443 405779

Enquiry form

For further details of any entry, post this form direct to the address listed. Please use block letters, and enclose a stamped addressed envelope or, if enquiring from outside the UK, an international reply coupon available from your local post office.

To:

(name of private house, guesthouse or hotel)

I have seen your entry in *Vegetarian Visitor*. Please send me details.

My name is:

Address:

Tel:

The dates I/we hope to stay with you are:
        from
        to
        (number of nights:)
I/we need
        _____ double room(s)
        _____ twin bedded room(s)
        _____ single room(s)
        _____ cot(s) for children aged _____

Other information or requests:

Signed:

Enquiry form

For further details of any entry, post this form direct to the address listed. Please use block letters, and enclose a stamped addressed envelope or, if enquiring from outside the UK, an international reply coupon available from your local post office.

To:

(name of private house, guesthouse or hotel)

I have seen your entry in *Vegetarian Visitor*. Please send me details.

My name is:

Address:

Tel:

The dates I/we hope to stay with you are:
      from
      to
      (number of nights:)
I/we need
      _____ double room(s)
      _____ twin bedded room(s)
      _____ single room(s)
      _____ cot(s) for children aged _____

Other information or requests:

Signed:

Enquiry form

For further details of any entry, post this form direct to the address listed. Please use block letters, and enclose a stamped addressed envelope or, if enquiring from outside the UK, an international reply coupon available from your local post office.

To:

(name of private house, guesthouse or hotel)

I have seen your entry in *Vegetarian Visitor*. Please send me details.

My name is:

Address:

Tel:

The dates I/we hope to stay with you are:
        from
        to
        (number of nights:)
I/we need
          _____ double room(s)
          _____ twin bedded room(s)
          _____ single room(s)
          _____ cot(s) for children aged _____

Other information or requests:

Signed:

BTA offices

Overseas readers: your nearest British Tourist Authority office will be pleased to send you general information on request. Here is a selection of the main offices.

AUSTRALIA
  BTA, 210 Clarence Street, Sydney, NSW 2000
BELGIUM
  BTA, Avenue Louise 306, 1050 Brussels
CANADA
  BTA, 111 Avenue Road, Suite 450, Toronto, Ontario, M5R 3J8
DENMARK
  BTA, Møntergade 3, 1116 Copenhagen K
FRANCE
  Tourisme de Grande-Bretagne, Maison de la Grande-Bretagne, 19 rue des Mathurins, 75009 Paris
GERMANY
  BTA, Taunusstraße 52-60, 60329 Frankfurt / Main
GREECE
  Action Public Relations, Kritonos 23, 161 21 Pangrati
HONG KONG
  Room 1504, Eton Tower, 8 Hysan Avenue, Causeway Bay
IRELAND
  BTA, 18–19 College Green, Dublin 2
ITALY
  BTA, Corso V. Emanuele II No 337, 00186 Rome
JAPAN
  BTA, Akasaka Twin Tower 1F, 2-17-22 Akasaka, Minato-ku, Tokyo 107
NETHERLANDS
  BTA, Aurora Gebouw, Stadhouderskade 2 (5e), 1054 ES Amsterdam
NEW ZEALAND
  BTA, 3rd Floor, Dilworth Building, Corner Queen & Customs Streets, Auckland 1
PORTUGAL
  BTA, Rua Luciano Cordeiro, 123 2°DT°, 1050 Lisbon
SINGAPORE
  BTA, 24 Raffles Place, # 19-06 Clifford Centre, 048621
SOUTH AFRICA
  BTA, Lancaster Gate, Hyde Lane, Hyde Park 2196. Post: P.O. Box 41896, Craighall 2024
SPAIN
  BTA, Torre de Madrid 6/5, Pza. de España, 28008 Madrid
SWEDEN
  BTA, Klara Norra, Kyrkogata 29, 111 22 Stockholm. Postal address: Box 745, 101 35 Stockholm
SWITZERLAND
  BTA, Limmatquai 78, 8001 Zürich
U.S.A.
  New York : BTA, 551 Fifth Avenue, Suite 701, New York NY 10176–0799
  Chicago: BTA, 625 North Michigan Avenue, Suite 1510, Chicago, IL 60611